Living Traditions

PATHFINDER EDITION

By Cristina G. Mittermeier, Jennifer Peters, and Cheryl Block

CONTENTS

2 Painted People

8 Huli Hair

10 Saving the World's Voices

12 Concept Check

Painted People

BY CRISTINA G. MITTERMEIER

Meet the people of Papua New Guinea.

Huli Hunters. *Huli men carry spears, bows, and arrows to hunt and to protect their families.*

On a large island in the South Pacific live some of the most diverse people in the world. They are the people of Papua New Guinea. They live in small groups, each with a different language and with different customs and beliefs. As a photographer, I have taken pictures of people all over the world, but it's these people I love best.

That's why I could barely contain my excitement as my friends and I floated up a river deep in the Papuan jungle. We were searching for a particular group of people called the Huli.

Soon, a village came into view. We looked for people, but we didn't see them. So we docked. I grabbed my camera and jumped out of the boat. Suddenly, painted faces surrounded me. The **indigenous people** welcomed me. Indigenous people are related to the first people in a place. As I greeted them, I thought about the thousands of years their ancestors have lived in this beautiful place.

Tribal Life

Though the country is no bigger than the state of California, more than 1,000 separate groups live in Papua New Guinea. Some do not get along with their neighbors. These groups have been at war for hundreds of years. There are disagreements about land, natural resources, and religious beliefs. Luckily, cliffs and jungles keep some groups apart. That helps to keep them from fighting.

Each group has a different culture, or way of life. It includes language, food, and more.

Learning about each culture helps me understand people. Take the Huli, for example. Men and women live apart, even when they are married. Men hunt and wear colorful wigs, while women do most of the work. Huli women raise kids, grow sweet potatoes, care for pigs, and help maintain their **community**.

Island Masterpieces

The center of that community is the spirit house. Spirit houses are some of the most important buildings in the Huli culture and most other cultures on the island. They are sacred places where people worship gods. In many groups, only men are allowed to go inside the spirit houses.

I am a woman, but I paid to go inside a spirit house. I did not have any idea what the inside of a spirit house would look like. What I saw inside stunned me. It was filled with beautiful objects, including shields, statues, and large hooks. Each one of them had been carefully painted. They were all amazing works of art.

Sacred Art. *These paintings decorate the inside of a spirit house.*

Lost in Translation

There are 850 languages spoken in Papua New Guinea, more than in any other country in the world. Still, I tried to communicate with people, despite not knowing their language. Sometimes, I didn't know what they were saying to me, which lead to confusion.

For example, I did not understand what one man was saying to me at a local market. He walked up to me carrying a poisonous plant covered with needles.

He smiled and rubbed the plant on my arm. Ouch! It stung. I did not know why he did that to me, but I acted like it did not hurt. He looked puzzled and walked away.

Still, most of the time, I was able to communicate fairly well. Through gestures and facial **expressions**, I could usually show people here how I felt and what I wanted. Luckily, I was usually able to understand them, too. That's important. Understanding how other people see the world helps me understand my own world better.

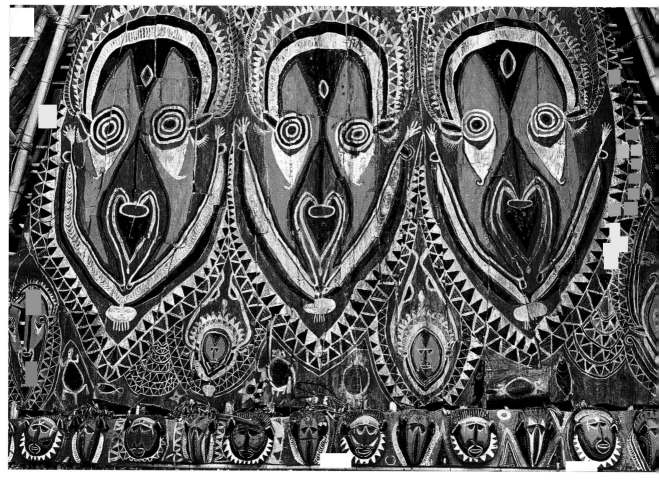

Colorful Dance. *These dancers show off their costumes at a festival on Mount Hagen.*

Fabulous Festivals

One morning at the end of my trip, I went to Mount Hagen, a tall mountain in the middle of Papua New Guinea. Some groups were having a **festival** there. I hoped they wouldn't mind that I invited myself to their big party.

More than 40,000 people went to the festival. They celebrated their past. They wore colorful costumes. They danced, told stories, and had fun for many days.

I walked around with my camera, snapping shot after shot. Drums thundered and feathers swayed. I saw people with great hats made out of ferns and other plants.

I saw some men who wore whitish grey body clay and spectacular masks made of mud. I saw Huli men with giant wigs decorated with colorful bird feathers.

Plenty of Photos

Soon a line formed near me. Painted people wanted me to take their pictures. I snapped photo after photo until I had gone through 100 rolls of film. I could not stop. The people were so beautiful.

The sun rose higher in the sky, and soon the light was too bright to take pictures. I put my camera away and walked into the crowd of painted people.

I tried to take in all the different sounds, smells, and colors of the day. Being surrounded by these strangers scared me a little; yet their smiles made me forget that I was far from home. We were all together, having fun. We were part of the same amazing planet.

Mud Men. *These men dress in masks made of mud for a festival. Their long claws are made of a plant called bamboo.*

HULI HAIR

BY JENNIFER PETERS

Hair Care. *Huli men wear mushroom-shaped wigs every day.*

Imagine if your future depended on having perfect hair. For teenage boys in the Huli culture, it does. Members of this remote group believe that hair shows a man's health and strength. Wearing elaborate wigs made from their own hair earns the respect of their people. So to Huli males, nothing is more important than growing great hair.

A HIDDEN PEOPLE

The Huli live deep in the rain forest of Papua New Guinea—an island nation north of Australia. They remained unknown to the outside world until the 1930s, when a gold rush brought explorers to their home. Today, about 70,000 people make up the Huli group. Most choose to follow their traditional way of life.

Where in the world is Papua New Guinea?

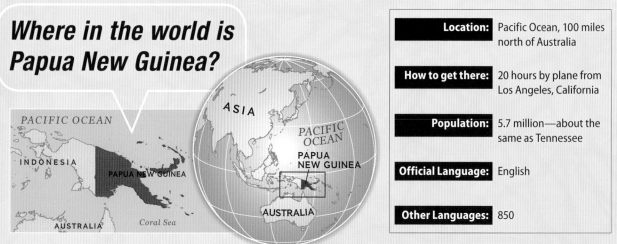

PACIFIC OCEAN

INDONESIA

PAPUA NEW GUINEA

AUSTRALIA   Coral Sea

ASIA

PACIFIC OCEAN

PAPUA NEW GUINEA

AUSTRALIA

Location:	Pacific Ocean, 100 miles north of Australia
How to get there:	20 hours by plane from Los Angeles, California
Population:	5.7 million—about the same as Tennessee
Official Language:	English
Other Languages:	850

TRADITIONS AND RULES

As teenagers, girls garden and babysit their younger siblings, while many boys go to wig school. Learning to grow their hair for wigs is an important tradition for these young men. The rules? 1) No running—you'll make your hair bounce; 2) Stay away from campfires; they could burn your hair; 3) Water your hair 12 times a day to make it grow faster. Breaking the rules could lead to suspension or even worse—bad hair!

BECOMING A MAN

Wearing wigs may seem strange to outsiders, but to the Huli, it has a much deeper meaning. When a Huli teen wears his first wig, it shows that he is strong enough for adult duties, such as warfare and marriage. To prepare, boys grow their hair for at least 18 months before cutting it. Wigmakers then weave the hair into mushroom-shaped headdresses for everyday wear. Boys add style with flowers and feathers. Later, they'll grow special wigs for ceremonies, taking their final steps toward becoming men.

Festival Face. *A young boy wears a feathered headdress and face paint for a special occasion.*

Huli Welcome. *A Huli tour guide introduces tourists to his culture.*

How would your life be different... if you were a Huli?

	LUNCH	HOBBIES	CHORES	FOR FUN
Kids in the U.S.	P B & J sandwich	Play soccer	Clean room	Play video games
Huli boys	Frogs and mice	Collect flowers and feathers for wig	Water hair	Play bamboo flute
Huli girls	Sweet potatoes	Weave string bags	Work in garden	Shop at outdoor market

Saving the World's Voices

By Cheryl Block

It is estimated that the world loses one language every 14 days.

National Geographic's Enduring Voices Project works to preserve endangered languages around the world. Researchers identify "hotspots"—places where the native languages are especially unique, poorly understood, or in danger of dying out.

Why is language so important? Many ancient people shared their traditions orally and never developed a written language. Once speakers of such languages are gone, we lose important knowledge of their cultures.

For example, Aboriginal Australian cultures are at least 50,000 years old. There are now only one or two remaining speakers of some of these cultures' languages. Researchers use modern technology to record the last remaining speakers. By preserving a people's language, we can also preserve its knowledge of the world.

NORTHWEST PACIFIC PLATEAU

OKLAHOMA-SOUTHWEST

MESOAMERICA

NORTHERN SOUTH AMERICA

CENTRAL SOUTH AMERICA

SOUTHERN SOUTH AMERICA

Yupik elders in the Arctic have separate words to describe 99 different types of sea ice. Modern scientists can learn a lot from their knowledge of the Arctic.

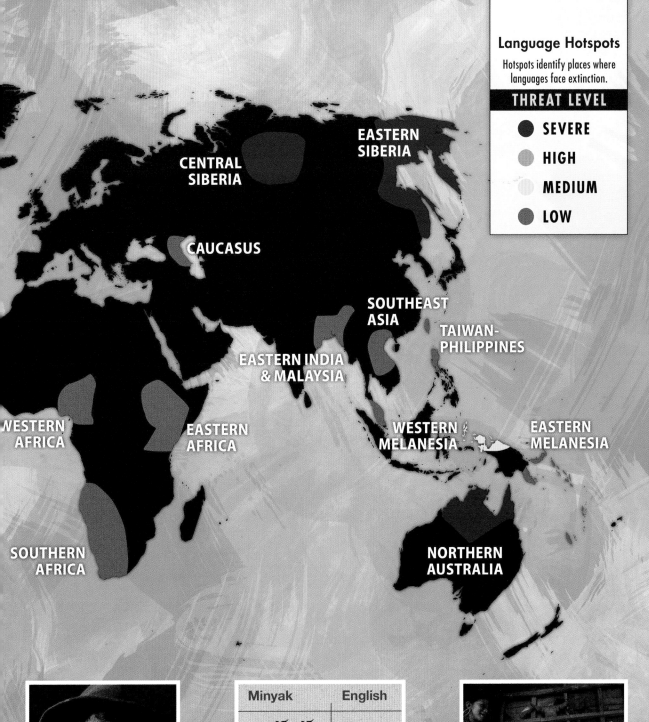

Language Hotspots

Hotspots identify places where languages face extinction.

THREAT LEVEL	
⚫	SEVERE
⚫	HIGH
⚫	MEDIUM
⚫	LOW

EASTERN SIBERIA

CENTRAL SIBERIA

CAUCASUS

SOUTHEAST ASIA

TAIWAN-PHILIPPINES

EASTERN INDIA & MALAYSIA

WESTERN AFRICA

EASTERN AFRICA

WESTERN MELANESIA

EASTERN MELANESIA

SOUTHERN AFRICA

NORTHERN AUSTRALIA

In Bolivia, the Kallawaya people protect their knowledge of medicinal plants by using a secret language that is known only in certain families.

Minyak	English
ནམ་སྐྱོན་པོ	blue sky
ཉི་མ	sun

This example of Minyak text shows another way to save a language. In Tibet, researchers created the first written form of an ancient language, Minyak. Community members then printed a Minyak textbook for local schools.

While recording endangered languages in India, researchers discovered a hidden language, Koro. It is spoken by only 800–1,200 people within a larger, 10,000-person tribe.

CULTURAL CONNECTIONS

Connect to other cultures by answering the questions below.

1 Why does Cristina Mittermeier try to talk with people when she does not know their language?

2 Cristina Mittermeier was welcomed by the indigenous people of Papua New Guinea. What does *indigenous* mean?

3 Why is wearing wigs for the first time an important tradition for Huli boys?

4 Why does the article say it is important to preserve the world's languages?

5 Is language important for understanding other cultures? Why or why not?